Unlocking The Power To Get Wealth

Understanding God's Plan for Spiritual & Financial Prosperity

Dr. Jacquelyn Hadnot

Unlocking The Power to Get Wealth

Unlocking The Power to Get Wealth

Dr. Jacquelyn Hadnot
Published by: Igniting the Fire Publishing
1314 North 38th Street
Kansas City, KS 66102
www.ignitingthefire.net

Unless otherwise noted, all Scripture quotations are taken from King James Version of the Bible.

Scripture quotations marked AMP are taken from The Amplified Bible AMP. The Amplified Bible, Old Testament copyright © 1965, 1987 by the Zondervan Corporation. The Amplified New Testament, copyright © 1954, 1958, 1987 by the Lockman Foundation. Used by permission.

Scripture quotations marked NASB are taken from The New American Standard Bible AMP. Copyright © 1960, 1962, 1963, 1968, 1971, 1972, 1973, 1975, 1977 by the Zondervan Corporation. The Amplified New Testament, copyright © 1954, 1958, 1987 by the Lockman Foundation. Used by permission.

Scripture quotations marked NIV are taken from The New International Version. Copyright © 1973, 1978, 1984 by the International Bible Society. Used by permission.

Please note that Igniting the Fire's publishing style capitalizes certain pronouns in Scripture that refer to the Father, Son, and Holy Spirit, and may differ from some Bible publishers' styles.

Unlocking The Power to Get Wealth

Table of Contents

Unlocking The Power to Get Wealth

Introduction

The Lord woke me at 3:00 a.m. with a word for His people. He spoke of wealth and the power needed to achieve wealth. The way in which we achieve wealth through Him in no way resembles what man thinks about achieving wealth.

In some cases, we are pursuing wealth contrary to the Lord's direction and instruction. We have begun a pursuit of wealth that is sure to lead many individuals down a road to destruction. Because of the selfish nature of many of wealth's trappings, we can find ourselves with a myriad of Satan's traps and certainly no favor from God.

I believe this book is a warning from the Lord to

His people. A warning of the dangers of pursuing worldly wealth at the cost of your salvation and discipleship. God wants to give us the fullness of His blessings, but we Must be in position if we are to receive from His hand. Pursuing worldly wealth at the expense of His favor is a high price to pay for things we cannot take with us. "For we brought nothing into this world, and it is certain we can carry nothing out" (1 Timothy 6:7).

The Lord is ready to pour out the wealth of the nations into the hand of His people, but He said, "we are not in the position." I pray that this book is a tool that the Lord uses to get us in position if we are to receive the wealth that He is ready to release into our hands.

People of God, it is time to get into position,

God's position and do what He is calling us to do in order to advance the Kingdom of God through the work, He has set before us. "Better the little that the righteous have than the wealth of many wicked; for the power of the wicked will be broken, but the LORD upholds the righteous." (Psalm 37:16-17). "And the wealth of the sinner is stored up for the righteous" (Proverbs 13:22).

1

Understanding the Power

The power to get wealth comes from God. It is not an earthly power. It is not a bought power. It is not a transferable power. It is from God and God alone.

Power of the Mind:

God gives you the ability to conceive an idea. Once an idea is conceived, next the desire to see it birthed out of the spiritual realm and into the natural realm.

Power of the Heart:

Next God impregnates your heart to believe that all things are possible if you believe in Him and His ability to transform your vision, desire or dream into reality. Believing and trusting Him for every direction to bring the vision to pass. The power of the heart is as strong as the power of the mind because they work in harmony, concerning the birth, believing the birth - there is nothing on earth that can stop you because you are operating under His power. He is giving you the ability to get wealth because of a promise He made to you and as long as you carry that promise in your heart, it will happen. When His power is flowing through your heart, you have more than enough to over come every hurdle that comes your way.

Power to Receive:

Walking the steps of conceiving and believing, guides you on the road to receive what God has for you. We receive from Him in many ways. We gain wisdom in order to build the vision. We receive knowledge on the right elements needed and have to operate in them and through them. We receive instruction for the path we must keep on if we are to see it happen. We receive motivation to sustain us when the enemy tries to distract us with fear, doubt or discouragement. We receive protection to keep us in all of our ways, so that the enemy cannot deceive us into miscarrying or aborting the vision. We receive patience to go the distance when the process seems delayed, halted or dead. Patience is essential because we don't want to push too soon and birth a deformed vision. Patience keeps us until it is the perfect timing of God to push forward. We receive peace to wait on the Lord when we are exhausted from carrying such a heavy load. We receive reminders that He is with us and are His chosen. He reminds us of the privilege of being His chosen. He doesn't impregnate everyone with the vision you were given. He reminds us of the price of being chosen, "so that the proof of your faith, being more precious than gold which is perishable, even though tested by fire, may be found to result in praise and glory and honor at the revelation of Jesus Christ" (1Peter 1:7). It is a price of holy, upright living and obedience. We receive strength when we are weak from the weight of our destiny. His strength brings us joy, peace, patience and more. The joy of the Lord truly is our strength. Finally, we receive love, Agape love. Even though things don't always look like we envision. His love guides us and keeps us on the journey alone. Because no one can carry the vision except you. Others can help you, but you must carry it alone. The love of God keeps us steady when we feel off balance.

Four steps in your power walk:
➤ Conceive
➤ Believe
➤ Receive
➤ Achieve

Power to Achieve:

You have walked out conceiving the vision; next you held onto the vision by believing the vision and received from the Lord what was needed to hold on through the trials and tribulations of carrying such a strong vision.

It is now time to achieve the vision that was spoken before the foundation of the world. Achieving it means you can see the physical manifestation of everything God spoke concerning your destiny and the vision. You can now see a spiritual promise in your natural realm. It is a reality both in the spiritual realm and in the natural. You birthed it out, and it is beautiful.

The Bible tells us that the wealth of the sinner is stored up for the righteous. The Spirit of the Lord said, "the wealth the Word of God speaks of is not always about money, daughter. Wealth also comes in the form of the knowledge that the world possesses. When that knowledge is taken and used for Kingdom purposes, it becomes a tool that will bring Me glory." He went on to say, "My people must stop equating wealth with money, otherwise they will miss one of the greatest wealth resources on earth - knowledge."

If you had millions of dollars, but did not possess the knowledge on how to handle it, you would be broke before the end of the year. Knowledge is power, and we must have wisdom and knowledge in every area of our lives.

We can acquire knowledge through education, but wisdom comes from God. You can have one hundred college degrees, but still possess no wisdom. There's an old saying, "There's nothing worse than an educated fool." It's sad, but it's true. Not all the training in the world can buy you the wisdom you need in order to advance in life.

Sometimes the highly educated believe that they achieved their high ranking or knowledge by their own strength. That is why we need to know that God gives His people power and the position they enjoy in life. It does not matter whether you have a title, position or education; humility is the ONLY posture you must take if you are to receive the God-given power to get wealth. I have more degrees than I want to mention, but God is not concerned with my degrees, He is concerned with my heart.

It is frightfully easy for an individual to fall prey to the bait of arrogance or pride when he or she accomplishes a goal or success if they are not walking in humility and acknowledging that God is the author of their success. The more a person takes credit for their accomplishments, the easier it is for the enemy to whisper "sweet nothings" in their ear convincing them that it was their power that brought the victory. This diminishes the power of God in their lives because God gives grace to the humble, but opposes the proud (James 4:6).

Humility is the only way when it comes to God's plan for you. Humility is the only solution when it comes to God's power working through you. Without humility, individuals will become like the children of Israel and say in their hearts, "My power and the might of my hands have gained me this wealth (Deuteronomy 8:17). The result, the individual is now walking in worldly wisdom, trying to achieve worldly wealth.

2

Worldly Wealth vs. Godly Wealth

Deuteronomy 8:18 tells us that it is God that gives us the power to get wealth. Many times worldly possessions are gained by means that are not of God, his principles or practices. This type of wealth should not be attributed to God. Satan will bless his own agenda when there is something he deceptively wants to achieve. Don't think that because a plan appears to be on track it is in the Lord's plan. Check with the Lord to make sure it is a part of His divine plan.

When you look at worldly wealth or the pursuit of it, you will find elements of greed in the background. Behind greed, you will find idolatry.

> "God gives us the power to get wealth."
>
> Deuteronomy 8:18

The demonic power associated with the desire for wealth and the pursuit of it often lead to bondage, "No one can serve two masters; for either he will hate the one and love the other, or he will be devoted to one and despise the other. You cannot serve God and wealth" (Matthew 6:24 NASB). Slaves have no power or authority; they end up trapped in a life of misery and pain.

Greed also opens a door for selfishness. This further diminishes the power of God in a person's life. The constant pursuit to amass wealth and resources can cause an individual to chase after "get rich quick schemes" such as:

✓ Buying into phony diamond mines

✓ Purchasing bogus stock

✓ Money Gifting

✓ Pyramid schemes

✓ Ponzi schemes

When greed and selfishness set in, people no longer find joy in advancing the Kingdom of God, but rather in themselves and their possessions. Once Satan has a individual operating in greed, selfishness and pride, the power of God stops flowing and the person is left operating under demonic influences. This in turn, opens doors for other Satan attacks. Satanic attacks trap the person in a relentless cycle of chasing after the agenda of the enemy. He or she then unwittingly becomes a instrument that the enemy can use to spread the deadly lies of Satan.

To avoid this we must examine our own heart and desires. How do you do this? By asking yourself:

- Am I a greedy person?
- Am I a selfish person?
- Do I hunger for wealth?
- Do I hunger for power and position?
- Do I long for the prestige that comes from wealth?
- Have I strayed from the vision God gave me and started chasing a *money god*?

Ask yourself honestly and openly these questions and let the Lord to bring you face to face with the enemy in you. Then ask God to show you what He sees in you. Pray Psalm 139 as you approach

God for the answer to each question.

"O LORD, You have searched me and known me. You know when I sit down and when I rise up; You understand my thought from afar. You scrutinize my path and my lying down, And are intimately acquainted with all my ways. Even before there is a word on my tongue, Behold, O LORD, You know it all. You have enclosed me behind and before, And laid Your hand upon me. Such knowledge is too wonderful for me; It is too high, I cannot attain to it. Where can I go from Your Spirit? Or where can I flee from Your presence? If I ascend to heaven, You are there; If I make my bed in Sheol, behold, You are there. If I take the wings of the dawn, If I dwell in the remotest part of the sea, Even there Your hand will lead me, And Your right hand will lay hold of me. If I say, "Surely the darkness will overwhelm me, And the light around me will be night," Even the darkness is not dark to You, And the night is as bright as the day. Darkness and light are alike to You. For You formed my inward parts; You wove me in my mother's womb. I will give thanks to You, for I am fearfully and wonderfully made; Wonderful are Your works, And my soul knows it very well. My frame was not hidden from You, When I was made in secret, And skillfully wrought in the depths of the earth; Your eyes have seen my unformed substance; And in Your book were all written The days that were ordained for me, When as yet there was not one of them. How precious also are Your thoughts to me, O God! How vast is the sum of them! If I should count them, they would outnumber the sand. When I awake, I am still with You. O that You would slay the wicked, O God; Depart from me, therefore, men of bloodshed. For they speak against You wickedly, And Your enemies take Your name in vain. Do I not hate those who hate You, O LORD? And do I not loathe those who rise up against You? I hate them with the utmost hatred; They have become my enemies. Search me, O God, and know my heart; Try me and know my anxious thoughts; And see if there be any hurtful way in me, And lead me in the everlasting way" (Psalm 139:1-24).

Unlocking The Power to Get Wealth

3

Money is Not Evil

Money is not the root of evil, the love of money is a cause of evil, "For the love of money is a root of all sorts of evil, and some by longing for it have wandered away from the faith and pierced themselves with many grief's" (1Timothy 6:10). Money in the wrong hands is like poison to the bones - it will eat away at the individual's ability to be discipled and ultimately their salvation. "Again I say to you, it is easier for a camel to go through the eye of a needle, than for a rich man to enter the kingdom of God" (Matthew 19:24).

How? By way of the following:

- **Riches can give a false sense of security.**

  "Beware, and be on your guard against every form of greed; for not even when one has an abundance does his life consist of his possessions" (Luke 12:15).

- **Riches can bring deception.**

  "And the one on whom seed was sown among the thorns, this is the man who hears the word, and the worry of the world and the deceitfulness of wealth choke the word, and it becomes unfruitful" (Matthew 13:22).

- **Riches demand total loyalty to the heart.**
"For where your treasure is, there your heart will be also" (Matthew 6:21).

- **Rich people sometimes live as if they don't need God.**
"The seed which fell among the thorns, these are the ones who have heard, and as they go on their way they are choked with worries and riches and pleasures of this life, and bring no fruit to maturity" (Luke 8:14).

- **People can be led into temptation and harmful desires.**
"But those who want to get rich fall into temptation and a snare and many foolish and harmful desires which plunge men into ruin and destruction" (1Timothy 6:9).

- **Riches can lead to abandoning the faith.**
"For the love of money is a root of all sorts of evil, and some by longing for it have wandered away from the faith and pierced themselves with many grief's" (1Timothy 6:10).

Money in the wrong hands can be a lethal weapon to a person's salvation. The Bible tells us that, no Christian should desire to get rich in First Timothy 6:9-11. The key word is DESIRE.

> Money in the wrong hands can be a lethal weapon.

Striving and pursuing wealth are a tool the enemy can use to alienate you from God. To desire something means to have a craving: a wish, or longing for something.

"But those who want to get rich fall into temptation, a snare, and many foolish and harmful desires, which plunge men into ruin and destruction. For the love of money is a root of all sorts of evil, and some by longing for it have wandered away from the faith and pierced themselves with many griefs. But flee from these things, you man of God, and pursue righteousness, godliness, faith, love, perseverance and gentleness" (1Timothy 6:9-11).

Money is a tool to be used to accomplish things in life. Your life's goal should never be to acquire money. It will become your "love", and that is a dangerous pursuit. What does money do when placed in the wrong hands? Money will enhance an person's weaknesses. "Whoever loves money never has money enough; whoever loves wealth is never satisfied with his income" (Ecclesiastes 5:10).

- If you love liquor, you'll be a drunk.
- If you love women, you'll be a whoremonger.
- If you love gambling, you'll be a gambler.
- If you are greedy, you will hoard possessions.

You must deal with your weaknesses before God starts to bless you. He is ready to reposition us for a transfer, but we must deal with our weaknesses now. There can be no further delays, souls are at stake, and the Kingdom is postured for the advancement by those who are ready to receive the transfer. That's why it is necessary to examine our motives when it comes to the desire for money.

4

Why Do You Do What You Do?

Why you do something determines what you do.
Look at First Timothy 6:3-10 and 17-19.

"If anyone advocates a different doctrine
and does not agree with sound words, those
of our Lord Jesus Christ, and with the
doctrine conforming to godliness, he is
conceited and understands nothing; but he
has a morbid interest in controversial
questions and disputes about words, out of
which arise envy, strife, abusive language,

evil suspicions and constant friction between men of depraved mind and deprived of the truth, who suppose that godliness is a means of gain. But godliness actually is a means of great gain when accompanied by contentment. For we have brought nothing into the world, so we cannot take anything out of it either. If we have food and covering, with these we shall be content. But those who want to get rich fall into temptation, a snare, and many foolish and harmful desires that plunge men into ruin and destruction. For the love of money is a root of all sorts of evil, and some by longing for it have wandered away from the faith and pierced themselves with many griefs" (1Timothy 6:3-10).

"Instruct those who are rich in this present world not to be conceited or to fix their hope on the uncertainty of riches, but on God, who richly supplies us with all things to enjoy. Instruct them to do good, to be rich in good works, to be generous and ready to share, storing up for themselves the treasure of a good foundation for the future, so that they may take hold of that which is life indeed" (1Timothy 6:17-19).

We are told that men of corrupt minds, destitute of the truth. believe that godliness is a "means of gain." This is evidence that their reason for being "godly" is the path to riches. WRONG MOTIVE! Verse 9 shows us that individuals who desire wealth fall into temptation, snares and into dangerous and foolish lusts that in turn drown

> Our motives will determine the direction we take. Wrong motives mean wrong direction.

them in ruins.

I have heard people say, "I just want to be rich." Or they claim, "I'll do anything to be rich." The enemy will use their passion, hunger or appetite for wealth as a trap that could destroy their life. Our motives will determine the direction we take. Wrong motives mean wrong direction. Right motives, right direction. Your motives are directly tied to the ability to get wealth. It is God who gives us the power to get wealth and He will not give His power to anyone operating with wrong motives.

The Apostle Paul taught us several things about wrong motives in First Timothy 6:3-10, 17-19:

- **The evidence of wrong motives** (v.3)

  If anyone advocates a different doctrine and does not agree with sound words, those of our Lord Jesus Christ, and with the doctrine conforming to godliness.

- **The nature of wrong motives** (vv. 4,5)

  He is conceited and understands nothing; but he has a morbid interest in controversial questions and disputes about words, out of which arise envy, strife, abusive language, evil suspicions, and constant friction between men of depraved mind and deprived of the truth, who suppose that godliness is a means of gain.

- **The result of wrong motives** (vv. 9.10)

  But those who want to get rich fall into temptation, a snare, and many foolish and harmful desires that plunge men into ruin and destruction. For the love of money is a root of all sorts of evil, and some by longing for it have wandered away from the faith and pierced themselves with many griefs.

We must examine our motives when it comes to money and possessions. We will never be used to the fullest if God cannot trust us with the riches of this world. "His lord said unto him, Well done, thou good and faithful servant: thou hast been faithful over a few things, I will make thee ruler over many things: enter thou into the joy of thy lord" (Matthew 25:21). It is imperative that we watch our motives. There are key principles we must adhere to when watching our motives.

1. Problems come when we want things for the wrong reasons.
2. A Godly lifestyle brings rewards, but the rewards must not control us.
3. Prosperity is everything above our basic needs of food and shelter.
4. We must learn to be content with what we have and where we are.
5. Wrong motive lead to wrong decisions.
6. Wrong decisions destroy the power of God working through us.
7. We must trust in the Lord for every step we take and every move we make.

Unlocking The Power to Get Wealth

5

What Activates The Power to Create Wealth?

Two elements activate the power to create wealth:

1. Living a life that invites the blessings of God.

2. Eliminating the **drains** that rob us of what we already have. A drain does two things: (1) it diminishes or uses up resources or energy, *a serious drain on our cash reserves* **(2)** the gradual loss, withdrawal, or diminishing of something regarded as an important resource.

In order to live a life that invites the blessings of God, we must eliminate the drains that rob us of what we already have. We must not be

> Living a life that invites the blessings of God

wasteful with the things God has entrusted to our stewardship. Finally, we must destroy any strongholds that diminish the power of God in our lives.

There are seven sins (strongholds) that will rob you of your ability to create wealth. Strongholds are dangerous and must be addressed, if we are to move into a place where we can be trusted with wealth. They are dangerous because they can kill, steal and destroy in the following seven areas:

1. **Spiritually:** relating to the soul or spirit, usually in contrast to material things.
2. **Mentally:** relating to, found in, or occurring in the mind
3. **Socially:** relating to the way in which we behave and interact with others.
4. **Economically:** with regard to economics or financial matters
5. **Psychologically:** relating to the mind or mental processes
6. **Emotionally:** relating to or expressing emotion: anger, depression
7. **Physically:** relating to your body or appearance

The seven sins (strongholds) that will rob you of your power to create wealth are:

1. **Pride**: Lies about the source of all blessings.

2. **Anger**: Keeps us from working at our best.

3. **Greed**: Creates financial stagnation.

4. **Lust**: Robs us of our strength and focus.

5. **Sloth**: Keeps us from sowing and reaping.

6. **Gluttony**: Causes us to consume all our seed.

7. **Envy**: Prevents us from seeing our own blessings.

The enemy has intrinsic (internal) and extrinsic (externals) weapons that are designed to kill and destroy your stability and ability to create wealth. Again, these weapons come against you through your emotions, finances, social, physical, psychological, interpersonal, spiritual, or organizational areas of life.

If we are to destroy the works of the enemy, we must pursue the things of God. We must make the God Confession...

Unlocking The Power to Get Wealth

6

Confession Brings Possession

First Timothy 6:11 tells us to pursue righteousness, godliness, faith, love, perseverance and gentleness. If we heed the words of the Apostle Paul, God's blessings will overtake us.

Look at Deuteronomy 8:18:

"But you shall remember the LORD your God, for it is *He who is giving you power to make wealth* that He may confirm His covenant which He swore to your fathers, as it is this day" (emphasis added).

Also look at Deuteronomy 6:10-19: "Then it shall come about when the LORD your God brings you into the land which He swore to your fathers, Abraham, Isaac and Jacob, to give you, great and splendid cities which you did not build, and houses full of all good things which you did not fill, and hewn cisterns which you did not dig, vineyards and olive trees which you did not plant, and you eat and are satisfied, then watch yourself, that you do not forget the LORD who brought you from the land of Egypt, out of the house of slavery. " You shall fear only the LORD your God; and you shall worship Him and swear by His name. "You shall not follow other gods, any of the gods of the peoples who surround you, for the LORD your God in the midst of you is a jealous God; otherwise the anger of the LORD your God will be kindled against you, and He will wipe you off the face of the earth. "You shall not put the LORD your God to the test, as you tested Him at Massah. "You should diligently keep the commandments of the LORD your God, and

> Money is not evil; it is the LOVE of money that is a root of overspending, hoarding, greed and other strongholds.

His testimonies and His statutes which He has commanded you. "You shall do what is right and good in the sight of the LORD, that it may be well with you and that you may go in and possess the good land which the LORD swore to give your fathers, by driving out all your enemies from before you, as the LORD has spoken."

Deuteronomy 6:10-19 speaks of the promise of God to bring His people into a wealthy place if we will not follow other gods nor put Him to the test. If we hold steadfast in our obedience to Him and diligently keep His commandments, His testimonies and His statutes and do what is right and good in His sight then it may be well with us and we may go in and possess the good land.

It is not a high price to pay to receive the blessings of the Lord. The power to create wealth comes from our obedience to the Lord. Possessing the land is tied to the power to create wealth. Once God's power is activated in your life, you can go in and possess the land.

Can you see in the scriptures above the power of the Lord working in the lives of His people who choose to obey Him? This is the power to create wealth! Not your title, position, socio-economic status, gender or race. It is God's power and His power alone.

Remember money is simply a tool to accomplish the necessary things in life. Money is not evil; it is the LOVE of money that is a root of overspending, hoarding, greed and other strongholds.

God is ready to pour out the wealth of the nations into the hands of His people, but He cannot because we ARE NOT IN POSITION. It is time to get in position and let the Lord to flow into us. It is our mandate to advance the Kingdom of God, and it is going to take resources to accomplish this monumental task. Therefore, we must be in position if God is to release the vast wealth of the nations into our hands. "He that is faithful in that which is least is faithful also in much: and he that is unjust in the least is unjust also in much. If therefore, ye have not been faithful in the unrighteous mammon, who will commit to your trust the true riches? And if ye have not been faithful in that which is another man's, who shall give you that which is your own? No servant can serve two masters: for either he will hate the one, and love the other; or else he will hold to the one, and despise the other. Ye cannot serve God and mammon" (Luke 16:13).

7

Understanding the Wealth of the World

"And the lord commended the unjust
steward, because he had done wisely:
for the children of this world are in their
generation wiser than the children of light."
(Luke 16:8)

"And the wealth of the sinner is stored
up for the righteous."
(Proverbs 13:22)

In prayer one night, the Lord spoke these words
regarding the wealth of the world. The Spirit of
the Lord said, "The wealth the Word speaks of is

not always about money, daughter. Wealth also comes in the form of the knowledge that the world possesses. When that knowledge is taken and used for Kingdom purposes, it becomes a tool that will bring Me glory." He went on to say, "My people must stop equating wealth with money, otherwise they will miss one of the greatest wealth resources on earth - knowledge."

> "And the wealth of the sinner is stored up for the righteous." (Proverbs 13:22)

Imagine taking the knowledge of this world, turning it around for the Kingdom of God. We would see a world utterly transformed in many areas. If we took the knowledge base of this world's system and used it for the good of all people we would be able to:

- Wipe out world hunger and poverty.

- Cure many diseases.

- Educate children around the world.

- Provide for the elderly and orphans.

- Provide financially for the poor.

- Make massive strides to end homelessness.

- Provide better employment opportunities.

- Stimulate the world's economy.

If we pooled the knowledge and other resources in countries around the world, we would see a world of peace, harmony and prosperity. The knowledge alone would end many of our planet's problems.

My idea of a way to end the housing crisis in America would look like the scenario below:

President Obama gave billions in bail out money to the automotive, banking and mortgage industries. Instead of giving that money to industry fat cats, what if he gave the money to the people that actually needed it, the American taxpayers. If he had distributed the bailout funds to every taxpaying citizen based on their federal income taxes, he could have given each citizen about $250,000. That type of bailout would pay off the mortgage on many middle class homes. Leaving each household virtually debt free, they would have more disposable income to put back into the economy. That my dear reader would be economic stimulation like never before. I firmly believe he bailed out the wrong people. Giving a lifeline to a person who already has one while leaving another person to drown is a sad state of affairs. When you look at the bailout of the Great

Recession that is exactly what President Obama did to the American people. He left us to drown.

Technologically, we are a well advanced society. With the Internet, advancements in medical treatments, and technological developments we are truly a modern society. Unfortunately, many of these areas are used to keep some sectors of society in a constant state of poverty and decay. Everyone would benefit if we took our advancements in technology and used it for the good of all people.

Greed has kept our world's systems in a holding pattern. Because of greed many men have gone to their graves leaving vast wealth in the hands of individuals with their same mindset. "For he sees that even wise men die; the [self-confident] fool and the stupid alike perish and leave their wealth to others. Their inward thought is that their houses will continue forever, and their dwelling places to all generations; they call their lands their own [apart from God] and after their own names. But man, with all his honor and pomp, does not remain; he is like the beasts that perish" (Psalm 49:10-12 AMP).

What Does this World Need?

This world needs wisdom in order to survive and thrive. We have individuals in positions that are for the most part, foolish. They are educated, well-traveled individuals, but they do not possess the wisdom to preserve and strengthen our nation. They possess a form of wisdom, but deny the power of the One who gives power. Therefore, they do not operate at their fullest potential. They make decisions based on selfish motives. "Of what use is money in the hand of a [self-confident] fool to buy skillful and godly Wisdom—when he has no understanding or heart for it?" (Proverbs 17:16 AMP). Furthermore, "Like a partridge that hatches eggs it did not lay is the man who gains riches by unjust means. When his life is half gone, they will desert him, and in the end he will prove to be a fool" (Jeremiah 17:11).

If we want different results, we must begin to do things differently. As a nation, we have been struggling for years. Existing and never advancing economically. As a nation we left our first love. We have removed God from the very fabric of this country. As a result, we have been thrown into a cistern of economic mire.

Constantly recycling ideas that never worked and rejecting new ideas that could change the fabric of the nation. Rejecting everything that is God. The only way to turn things around is to begin to seek Godly wisdom for the answers we need. "But if any of you lacks wisdom, let him ask of God, who gives to all generously and without reproach, and it will be given to him" (James 1:5).

Wisdom will be our only protection against the traps and snares of the enemy. Money has a field of protection, but wisdoms field of protection is infinite. Wisdom will preserve the life of this country, and it's people. Wisdom will allow us the edge over people and countries that operate outside of God's wisdom and protection. "For wisdom is protection just as money is protection,

But the advantage of knowledge is that wisdom preserves the lives of its possessors (Ecclesiastes 7:12).

What is the outcome of the foolishly confident? What happens to an economic system that turns its back on God? What happens to the people when they reject the wisdom of God? Destruction.

"For the wisdom of this world is foolishness before God" (1 Corinthians 3:19). This is the fate of those who are foolishly confident. Selah [pause, and calmly think of that]! (Psalm 49:13a).

Unlocking The Power to Get Wealth

8

Trusting God for the Power to Get Wealth

The Bible tells us in Proverbs 3:5, "Trust in the LORD with all your heart and do not lean on your own understanding. In all your ways acknowledge Him, And He will make your paths straight. Do not be wise in your own eyes; Fear the LORD and turn away from evil." Trusting and obeying the Lord is the only way to create the wealth He desires to give us.

Trust, faith and obedience, will activate the power to create wealth in your life. When His power is flowing through you, you have more than enough to over come every hurdle that comes your way.

When you walk out the steps of conceiving, believing, receiving and achieving, in addition to your obedience, you are positioning yourself to possess the land. "Oh, the depth of the riches both of the wisdom and knowledge of God! How unsearchable are His judgments and unfathomable His ways" (Romans 11:33)!

God is ready to pour out the wealth of the nations into the hands of His people, therefore, let us get IN POSITION. It is time to get in position, posture ourselves, and allow the Lord to flow into us. Therefore, we must come in alignment with God so that He will release the vast wealth of the nations into our hands. Trust, obedience and faith, will stir the heart of God on your behalf. "Now it shall be, if you diligently obey the LORD your God, being careful to do all His commandments

> God is ready to pour out the wealth of the nations into the hands of HIS people, therefore let's get IN POSITION.

which I command you today, the LORD your God will set you high above all the nations of the earth." "All these blessings will come upon you and overtake you if you obey the LORD your God: "Blessed shall you be in the city, and blessed shall you be in the country. "Blessed shall be the offspring of your body and the produce of your ground and the offspring of your beasts, the increase of your herd and the young of your flock. "Blessed shall be your basket and your kneading bowl. "Blessed shall you be when you come in, and blessed shall you be when you go out. "The LORD shall cause your enemies who rise against you to be defeated before you; they will come out against you one way and will flee before you seven ways. "The LORD will command the blessing upon you in your barns and in all that you put your hand to, and He will bless you in the land which the LORD your God gives you. "The LORD will establish you as a holy people to Himself, as He swore to you if you keep the commandments of the LORD your God and walk in His ways" (Deuteronomy 28:9).

The Lord is ready to establish His people in ways that we cannot believe. Our requirement is to get in position and walk in His ways. Stand unmovable and steadfast in His ways. In this season, He is ready to give you the power to get the wealth needed to advance the Kingdom of God.

Unlocking The Power to Get Wealth

9

Conclusion

We have come to the end of our journey, and you now know that this book had nothing to do with the natural aspects of telling you how to obtain money, land, or properties (I teach that subject in my Financial Management classes). It had nothing to do with the world's aspects of attaining wealth. This book was written to open your heart and mind to the season of possession. Thereby enabling you to access the power of God in every area of your life. When the power of

God is flowing through you, the Bible tells us in Psalm 84:11, "No good thing does He withhold from those who walk uprightly." When you walk in God's power and favor, there is nothing that will be withheld from you. That is a promise from God that you can stand on. When the favor of God is on your life, you will not have to beg and plead; all you have to do is trust and believe. God told the Israelites to "go in and possess the land." When God

> "No good thing does He withhold from those who walk uprightly."
> Psalm 84:11

commands you to "go in and possess the land", it is up to you to walk through the doors that he opens for you. It is up to you to remain in a place of obedience, fasting, prayer, humility and total submission to His will. It is up to you to stay on your face before Him for the plans and directions for the journey. God will not force you to obey just as He will not force you to meet the requirements in order to receive your blessings.

We should be like Solomon, instead of asking for money, cars, land and property; we should ask the Lord for the wisdom to manage our blessings before we receive them. King Solomon asked for wisdom, not only did God grant his request, Solomon received a wealth beyond measure. It is time to stop chasing money, fortune or popularity and start chasing after the giver of every good and perfect gift. It is time to chase after God. When you seek God Almighty, El Shaddai, you will catch Him and the blessings and unmerited favor of God will begin to chase you. Then you will know without a doubt that you have the POWER TO GET WEALTH!

Beloved, I pray that in all respects you may prosper and be in good health, just as your soul prospers.

3 John 1:2

Prayer of Deliverance

Heavenly Father, I repent of any sins in my life or my ancestors' lives that have resulted in a curse. I repent of all disobedience, rebellion, perversion, witchcraft, idolatry, lust, adultery, fornication, mistreatment of others, murder, cheating, lying, sorcery, divination, and occult involvement. I ask for Your forgiveness and cleansing through the blood of the Lord Jesus Christ.

I take authority over and break any and every curse upon my life in the Name of Jesus. I break all curses of poverty, lack, debt, destruction, sickness, death, and vagabondism. I break all curses on my marriage, family, children, and relationships. I break curses of rejection, pride, rebellion, lust, hurt, incest, rape, Ahab, Jezebel, fear, insanity, madness, and confusion.

I break all curses affecting my finances, mind, sexual character, emotions, will, and relationships.

I break every jinx, hex, spell and spoken curse over my life.

I break every fetter, shackle, chain, cord, habit, and cycle that is the result of a curse.

According to Galatians 3:13, I have been redeemed from *"the curse of the law"* by the sacrifice of Jesus. I exercise my faith in the blood of Jesus and loose my descendants and myself from any and every curse. I claim forgiveness through the blood of Jesus for the sins of the fathers.

All my sins have been remitted, and I loose myself from the curses that came as a result of all disobedience and rebellion to the Word of God.

I exercise my faith, and I know that confession is made unto salvation (Romans 10:10). Therefore, I confess that Abraham's blessings are mine (Galatians 3:14). I am not cursed, but blessed. I am *"the head, and not the tail"* (Deuteronomy 28:13). I am blessed coming in and blessed going out. I am blessed, and what God has blessed cannot be cursed.

I command spirits of rejection, hurt, bitterness, unforgiveness, bondage, torment, death, destruction, fear, lust, perversion, mind control, witchcraft, poverty, lack, debt, confusion, double-mindlessness, sickness, infirmity, pain, divorce, separation, loneliness, self-pity, self-destruction, [1]

self-rejection, anger, rage, wrath, anguish, vagabondism, abuse, and addiction to come out in the name of Jesus!

Lord, I thank you for setting me free from every curse and every spirit that has operated in my life as a result of a curse. Amen.

Bínð My Mínð to the Will of Goð

Heavenly Father, In the Name and authority of Jesus Christ and by the power of His shed Blood, I come to You now as I bind my mind to the will of God, I bind _____ mind to the will of God in the Name of Jesus Christ. Romans 12:2 tells us to not conform any longer to the pattern of this world, but be transformed by the renewing of my mind. Then I will be able to test and approve what God's will is—his good, pleasing and perfect will. Heavenly Father, in the name of Jesus, I ask you to transform my mind into Your mind. In the Name of Jesus, I pray with thanksgiving. Amen.

Unlocking The Power to Get Wealth

About the Author

God has called Jacquie Hadnot to encourage, inspire, motivate and activate the gifts of the Spirit in order to birth powerful ministries in the body of Christ. She is becoming a voice on the subject of prayer, worship and spiritual warfare.

She is recognized as a modern-day apostle with a strong prophetic and psalmist anointing. She has a revelational teaching ministry with a mandate to saturate the world with the Word of God. Jacquies heart is to see people rise and walk in the destiny and inheritance of the Lord.

She has founded and established It Is Written Ministries, a publication company, an accounting and consulting firm, and a global radio station. As a retired accountant and business executive, Jacquie blends ministerial and entrepreneurial applications in her ministry to enrich and empower a diverse audience with skills and abilities to take kingdoms for the Lord Jesus Christ. She is a lecturer, conference speaker, teacher, business trainer, and financial consultant, providing consulting services to businesses, churches, and individuals. She has written over twenty-five books, manuals, and other materials on intimacy with God, prayer, fasting and spiritual warfare. She has also released several music Cds and received numerous music and book publishing awards.

Beyond the pulpit, Jacquie is a talk show host on both television and radio with her own program, Light for Your Path. Weekly she applies God's wisdom to today's world solutions. Her ministry objective is to make Christ's teachings relevant for today. She also publishes a quarterly magazine by the same name.

In addition to her extensive experience, Jacquie has a Thd in Pastoral Theology and a Masters in Ministry Leadership. She is also a wife, mother of one daughter and grandmother of one grandson. She and her husband, Gregory presently pastor It Is Written Ministries in Kansas City Kansas. They also serve as owners and officers of Igniting the Fire Media Group.

Unlocking The Power to Get Wealth

Unlocking The Power to Get Wealth

Other Books & Materials by Dr. Jacquie

Books in Print

- The Art of Spiritual Warfare: Strategies for Effective Warfare
- A Woman of Worth: Loving the Skin I'm In
- A Woman of Worth: From Victim to Victor
- There's A Famine in the Land: *Overcoming Great Recession*
- Your Declaration of Dependence on God
- Closing the Doors to Satan's Attacks: *Overcoming Fear*
- Trapped in the Arms of Death: *Overcoming Grip of Suicide*
- The Extravagant Love of God: Experiencing the Prophetic Flow
- Cry Aloud, Spare Not! A Prophetic Call to Fast God Has Chosen
- Cry Aloud, Spare Not! The Companion-Study Guide
- His Mercy Endures Forever: Psalms, Prayers & Meditations
- To Make War with the Saints; Satan's Kingdom Agenda
- A Treasure in the Pleasure of Loving God
- Loving God through His Names: 365 Days of the Year
- Where Is Your God? Have We Lost Referential Fear of the Lord?
- When Fear Crept In
- Deeper...
- Naked, Broken and Unashamed

Audio Books & Teachings

➤ More of You… (Volume 1)

➤ In the Face of Adversity: *Overcoming Life's Storms*

➤ Be Not Deceived…

➤ Where Is Your God?

➤ Recognizing Your Due Season

➤ Praying the Healing Scriptures

➤ The Enemy in Me: *Overcoming Self-Life Issues*

➤ Trusting God in a Season of Discouragement

➤ The Harlot Heart

Music

➤ The Extravagant Love of God

➤ The Spoken Word of Love

➤ His Mercy Endures Forever: Praying the Psalms

DVD

➤ When Your Faith is Being Tested

➤ What Made David Run

➤ Agents of Change

➤ Virtuous Women of Worship

TO CONTACT DR. JACQUIE
www.jacquiehadnot.com
www.ignitingthefire.net
Or write us:
jacquie@jacquiehadnot.com

Also available

A Woman of Worth: Loving the Skin I'm In

A Woman of Worth Study Guide
A comprehensive study guide designed to reinforce the teachings from the book and the conference.

A Woman of Worth Journal
To help you on your journey of discovering the woman God pre-destined you to be. Journaling is a great way to keep your thoughts and meditations on paper.

A Woman of Worth: From Victim to Victor

Coming Soon!

A Woman of Worth Audio Book
A Woman of Worth E-Book

_____

_____

_____

_____

_____

_____

_____

_____

_____

_____

_____

_____

_____

_____

_____

_____

_____

_____

_____

_____
_____
_____
_____
_____
_____
_____
_____
_____
_____
_____
_____
_____
_____
_____
_____
_____
_____
_____
_____

_____

_____

_____

_____

_____

_____

_____

_____

_____

_____

_____

_____

_____

_____

_____

_____

_____

_____

_____

_____

_____

_____

_____

_____

_____

_____

_____

_____

_____

_____

_____

_____

_____

_____

_____

_____

_____

_____

_____

_____

_____

Unlocking The Power to Get Wealth

_____

_____

_____

_____

_____

_____

_____

_____

_____

_____

_____

_____

_____

_____

_____

_____

_____

_____

_____

_____

_____

_____

_____

_____

_____

_____

_____

_____

_____

_____

_____

_____

_____

_____

_____

_____

_____

_____

_____

_____

_____

_____

_____

_____

_____

_____

_____

_____

_____

_____

_____

_____

_____

_____

_____

_____

_____

_____

_____

_____

_____

_____

_____

_____

_____

_____

_____

_____

_____

_____

_____

_____

_____

_____

_____

_____

Unlocking The Power to Get Wealth

Unlocking The Power to Get Wealth

[1] [21] John Eckhardt, Identifying and Breaking Curses (Whitaker House 1999) pp.48.

Unlocking The Power to Get Wealth

www.ingramcontent.com/pod-product-compliance
Lightning Source LLC
Chambersburg PA
CBHW060632210326
41520CB00010B/1568